This book belongs to:

_____

_____

My jourey started on
this date:

_____

My reason for starting
my journey:

_____

_____

_____

DATE

Daily Journal

BREAKFAST

LUNCH

DINNER

SUPPLEMENTS/VITAMINS

SNACKS

WATER INTAKE

CALORIES   FATS   PROTEIN   CARBS

EXERCISE

DAILY REFLECTION

SLEEP

ENERGY LEVELS

DATE

Daily Journal

BREAKFAST

LUNCH

DINNER

SUPPLEMENTS/VITAMINS

SNACKS

WATER INTAKE

CALORIES   FATS   PROTEIN   CARBS

EXERCISE

DAILY REFLECTION

SLEEP

ENERGY LEVELS

DATE

Daily Journal

BREAKFAST

LUNCH

DINNER

SUPPLEMENTS/VITAMINS

SNACKS

WATER INTAKE

CALORIES   FATS   PROTEIN   CARBS

EXERCISE

DAILY REFLECTION

SLEEP

ENERGY LEVELS

DATE

Daily Journal

BREAKFAST

LUNCH

DINNER

SUPPLEMENTS/VITAMINS

SNACKS

WATER INTAKE

CALORIES   FATS   PROTEIN   CARBS

EXERCISE

DAILY REFLECTION

SLEEP

ENERGY LEVELS

DATE

Daily Journal

BREAKFAST

LUNCH

DINNER

SUPPLEMENTS/VITAMINS

SNACKS

WATER INTAKE

CALORIES   FATS   PROTEIN   CARBS

EXERCISE

DAILY REFLECTION

SLEEP

ENERGY LEVELS

DATE

Daily Journal

BREAKFAST

LUNCH

DINNER

SUPPLEMENTS/VITAMINS

SNACKS

WATER INTAKE

CALORIES   FATS   PROTEIN   CARBS

EXERCISE

DAILY REFLECTION

SLEEP

ENERGY LEVELS

DATE

Daily Journal

BREAKFAST

LUNCH

DINNER

SUPPLEMENTS/VITAMINS

SNACKS

WATER INTAKE

CALORIES   FATS   PROTEIN   CARBS

EXERCISE

DAILY REFLECTION

SLEEP

ENERGY LEVELS

Weekly Measurements Log

DATE

WEIGHT

CHEST

WAIST

BUTT

THIGHS

ARMS

HIPS

BMI

Photos During My Journey

INCLUDE PHOTOS DURING CELEBRATIONS AND MILESTONES!

Thoughts About The Week

Proud Moments

Lessons Leanred or Things I Can Do Better

In two weeks,
you'll feel it.
In four weeks,
you'll see it.
In eight weeks,
you'll hear it.

DATE

Daily Journal

BREAKFAST

LUNCH

DINNER

SUPPLEMENTS/VITAMINS

SNACKS

WATER INTAKE

CALORIES   FATS   PROTEIN   CARBS

EXERCISE

DAILY REFLECTION

SLEEP

ENERGY LEVELS

DATE

Daily Journal

BREAKFAST

LUNCH

DINNER

SUPPLEMENTS/VITAMINS

SNACKS

WATER INTAKE

CALORIES   FATS   PROTEIN   CARBS

EXERCISE

DAILY REFLECTION

SLEEP

ENERGY LEVELS

DATE

Daily Journal

BREAKFAST

LUNCH

DINNER

SUPPLEMENTS/VITAMINS

SNACKS

WATER INTAKE

CALORIES   FATS   PROTEIN   CARBS

EXERCISE

DAILY REFLECTION

SLEEP

ENERGY LEVELS

DATE

Daily Journal

BREAKFAST

LUNCH

DINNER

SUPPLEMENTS/VITAMINS

SNACKS

WATER INTAKE

CALORIES   FATS   PROTEIN   CARBS

EXERCISE

DAILY REFLECTION

SLEEP

ENERGY LEVELS

DATE

Daily Journal

BREAKFAST

LUNCH

DINNER

SUPPLEMENTS/VITAMINS

SNACKS

WATER INTAKE

CALORIES   FATS   PROTEIN   CARBS

EXERCISE

DAILY REFLECTION

SLEEP

ENERGY LEVELS

DATE

Daily Journal

BREAKFAST

LUNCH

DINNER

SUPPLEMENTS/VITAMINS

SNACKS

WATER INTAKE

CALORIES   FATS   PROTEIN   CARBS

EXERCISE

DAILY REFLECTION

SLEEP

ENERGY LEVELS

DATE

Daily Journal

BREAKFAST

LUNCH

DINNER

SUPPLEMENTS/VITAMINS

SNACKS

WATER INTAKE

CALORIES   FATS   PROTEIN   CARBS

EXERCISE

DAILY REFLECTION

SLEEP

ENERGY LEVELS

Weekly Measurements Log

DATE

WEIGHT

CHEST

WAIST

BUTT

THIGHS

ARMS

HIPS

BMI

Photos During My Journey

INCLUDE PHOTOS DURING CELEBRATIONS AND MILESTONES!

Thoughts About The Week

Proud Moments

Lessons Learned or Things I Can Do Better

If you are persistent, you will get it. If you are consistent, you will keep it.

DATE

Daily Journal

BREAKFAST

LUNCH

DINNER

SUPPLEMENTS/VITAMINS

SNACKS

WATER INTAKE

CALORIES   FATS   PROTEIN   CARBS

EXERCISE

DAILY REFLECTION

SLEEP

ENERGY LEVELS

DATE

Daily Journal

BREAKFAST

LUNCH

DINNER

SUPPLEMENTS/VITAMINS

SNACKS

WATER INTAKE

CALORIES   FATS   PROTEIN   CARBS

EXERCISE

DAILY REFLECTION

SLEEP

ENERGY LEVELS

DATE

Daily Journal

BREAKFAST

LUNCH

DINNER

SUPPLEMENTS/VITAMINS

SNACKS

WATER INTAKE

CALORIES   FATS   PROTEIN   CARBS

EXERCISE

DAILY REFLECTION

SLEEP

ENERGY LEVELS

DATE

Daily Journal

BREAKFAST

LUNCH

DINNER

SUPPLEMENTS/VITAMINS

SNACKS

WATER INTAKE

CALORIES   FATS   PROTEIN   CARBS

EXERCISE

DAILY REFLECTION

SLEEP

ENERGY LEVELS

DATE

Daily Journal

BREAKFAST

LUNCH

DINNER

SUPPLEMENTS/VITAMINS

SNACKS

WATER INTAKE

CALORIES   FATS   PROTEIN   CARBS

EXERCISE

DAILY REFLECTION

SLEEP

ENERGY LEVELS

DATE

Daily Journal

BREAKFAST

LUNCH

DINNER

SUPPLEMENTS/VITAMINS

SNACKS

WATER INTAKE

CALORIES   FATS   PROTEIN   CARBS

EXERCISE

DAILY REFLECTION

SLEEP

ENERGY LEVELS

DATE

Daily Journal

BREAKFAST

LUNCH

DINNER

SUPPLEMENTS/VITAMINS

SNACKS

WATER INTAKE

CALORIES   FATS   PROTEIN   CARBS

EXERCISE

DAILY REFLECTION

SLEEP

ENERGY LEVELS

Weekly Measurements Log

DATE

WEIGHT

CHEST

WAIST

BUTT

THIGHS

ARMS

HIPS

BMI

Photos During My Journey

INCLUDE PHOTOS DURING CELEBRATIONS AND MILESTONES!

Thoughts About The Week

Proud Moments

Lessons Learned or Things I Can Do Better

May the next few months be a period of magnificent transformation.

DATE

Daily Journal

BREAKFAST

LUNCH

DINNER

SUPPLEMENTS/VITAMINS

SNACKS

WATER INTAKE

CALORIES   FATS   PROTEIN   CARBS

EXERCISE

DAILY REFLECTION

SLEEP

ENERGY LEVELS

DATE

Daily Journal

BREAKFAST

LUNCH

DINNER

SUPPLEMENTS/VITAMINS

SNACKS

WATER INTAKE

CALORIES   FATS   PROTEIN   CARBS

EXERCISE

DAILY REFLECTION

SLEEP

ENERGY LEVELS

DATE

Daily Journal

BREAKFAST

LUNCH

DINNER

SUPPLEMENTS/VITAMINS

SNACKS

WATER INTAKE

CALORIES   FATS   PROTEIN   CARBS

EXERCISE

DAILY REFLECTION

SLEEP

ENERGY LEVELS

DATE

Daily Journal

BREAKFAST

LUNCH

DINNER

SUPPLEMENTS/VITAMINS

SNACKS

WATER INTAKE

CALORIES   FATS   PROTEIN   CARBS

EXERCISE

DAILY REFLECTION

SLEEP

ENERGY LEVELS

DATE

Daily Journal

BREAKFAST

LUNCH

DINNER

SUPPLEMENTS/VITAMINS

SNACKS

WATER INTAKE

CALORIES   FATS   PROTEIN   CARBS

EXERCISE

DAILY REFLECTION

SLEEP

ENERGY LEVELS

DATE

Daily Journal

BREAKFAST

LUNCH

DINNER

SUPPLEMENTS/VITAMINS

SNACKS

WATER INTAKE

CALORIES   FATS   PROTEIN   CARBS

EXERCISE

DAILY REFLECTION

SLEEP

ENERGY LEVELS

DATE

Daily Journal

BREAKFAST

LUNCH

DINNER

SUPPLEMENTS/VITAMINS

SNACKS

WATER INTAKE

CALORIES   FATS   PROTEIN   CARBS

EXERCISE

DAILY REFLECTION

SLEEP

ENERGY LEVELS

Weekly Measurements Log

DATE

WEIGHT

CHEST

WAIST

BUTT

THIGHS

ARMS

HIPS

BMI

Photos During My Journey

INCLUDE PHOTOS DURING CELEBRATIONS AND MILESTONES!

Thoughts About The Week

Proud Moments

Lessons Leanred or Things I Can Do Better

Your desire to change must be greater than your desire to stay the same.

DATE

Daily Journal

BREAKFAST

LUNCH

DINNER

SUPPLEMENTS/VITAMINS

SNACKS

WATER INTAKE

CALORIES   FATS   PROTEIN   CARBS

EXERCISE

DAILY REFLECTION

SLEEP

ENERGY LEVELS

DATE

Daily Journal

BREAKFAST

LUNCH

DINNER

SUPPLEMENTS/VITAMINS

SNACKS

WATER INTAKE

CALORIES   FATS   PROTEIN   CARBS

EXERCISE

DAILY REFLECTION

SLEEP

ENERGY LEVELS

DATE

Daily Journal

BREAKFAST

LUNCH

DINNER

SUPPLEMENTS/VITAMINS

SNACKS

WATER INTAKE

CALORIES   FATS   PROTEIN   CARBS

EXERCISE

DAILY REFLECTION

SLEEP

ENERGY LEVELS

DATE

Daily Journal

BREAKFAST

LUNCH

DINNER

SUPPLEMENTS/VITAMINS

SNACKS

WATER INTAKE

CALORIES   FATS   PROTEIN   CARBS

EXERCISE

DAILY REFLECTION

SLEEP

ENERGY LEVELS

DATE

Daily Journal

BREAKFAST

LUNCH

DINNER

SUPPLEMENTS/VITAMINS

SNACKS

WATER INTAKE

CALORIES   FATS   PROTEIN   CARBS

EXERCISE

DAILY REFLECTION

SLEEP

ENERGY LEVELS

DATE

Daily Journal

BREAKFAST

LUNCH

DINNER

SUPPLEMENTS/VITAMINS

SNACKS

WATER INTAKE

CALORIES   FATS   PROTEIN   CARBS

EXERCISE

DAILY REFLECTION

SLEEP

ENERGY LEVELS

DATE

Daily Journal

BREAKFAST

LUNCH

DINNER

SUPPLEMENTS/VITAMINS

SNACKS

WATER INTAKE

CALORIES   FATS   PROTEIN   CARBS

EXERCISE

DAILY REFLECTION

SLEEP

ENERGY LEVELS

Weekly Measurements Log

DATE

WEIGHT

CHEST

WAIST

BUTT

THIGHS

ARMS

HIPS

BMI

Photos During My Journey

INCLUDE PHOTOS DURING CELEBRATIONS AND MILESTONES!

Thoughts About The Week

Proud Moments

Lessons Learned or Things I Can Do Better

Don't wait for tomorrow. It may be one day too late.

DATE

Daily Journal

BREAKFAST

LUNCH

DINNER

SUPPLEMENTS/VITAMINS

SNACKS

WATER INTAKE

CALORIES   FATS   PROTEIN   CARBS

EXERCISE

DAILY REFLECTION

SLEEP

ENERGY LEVELS

DATE

Daily Journal

BREAKFAST

LUNCH

DINNER

SUPPLEMENTS/VITAMINS

SNACKS

WATER INTAKE

CALORIES   FATS   PROTEIN   CARBS

EXERCISE

DAILY REFLECTION

SLEEP

ENERGY LEVELS

DATE

Daily Journal

BREAKFAST

LUNCH

DINNER

SUPPLEMENTS/VITAMINS

SNACKS

WATER INTAKE

CALORIES   FATS   PROTEIN   CARBS

EXERCISE

DAILY REFLECTION

SLEEP

ENERGY LEVELS

DATE

Daily Journal

BREAKFAST

LUNCH

DINNER

SUPPLEMENTS/VITAMINS

SNACKS

WATER INTAKE

CALORIES   FATS   PROTEIN   CARBS

EXERCISE

DAILY REFLECTION

SLEEP

ENERGY LEVELS

DATE

Daily Journal

BREAKFAST

LUNCH

DINNER

SUPPLEMENTS/VITAMINS

SNACKS

WATER INTAKE

CALORIES   FATS   PROTEIN   CARBS

EXERCISE

DAILY REFLECTION

SLEEP

ENERGY LEVELS

DATE

Daily Journal

BREAKFAST

LUNCH

DINNER

SUPPLEMENTS/VITAMINS

SNACKS

WATER INTAKE

CALORIES   FATS   PROTEIN   CARBS

EXERCISE

DAILY REFLECTION

SLEEP

ENERGY LEVELS

DATE

Daily Journal

BREAKFAST

LUNCH

DINNER

SUPPLEMENTS/VITAMINS

SNACKS

WATER INTAKE

CALORIES   FATS   PROTEIN   CARBS

EXERCISE

DAILY REFLECTION

SLEEP

ENERGY LEVELS

Weekly Measurements Log

DATE

WEIGHT

CHEST

WAIST

BUTT

THIGHS

ARMS

HIPS

BMI

Photos During My Journey

INCLUDE PHOTOS DURING CELEBRATIONS AND MILESTONES!

Thoughts About The Week

Proud Moments

Lessons Leanred or Things I Can Do Better

Excuses don't get results.

DATE

Daily Journal

BREAKFAST

LUNCH

DINNER

SUPPLEMENTS/VITAMINS

SNACKS

WATER INTAKE

CALORIES   FATS   PROTEIN   CARBS

EXERCISE

DAILY REFLECTION

SLEEP

ENERGY LEVELS

DATE

Daily Journal

BREAKFAST

LUNCH

DINNER

SUPPLEMENTS/VITAMINS

SNACKS

WATER INTAKE

CALORIES   FATS   PROTEIN   CARBS

EXERCISE

DAILY REFLECTION

SLEEP

ENERGY LEVELS

DATE

Daily Journal

BREAKFAST

LUNCH

DINNER

SUPPLEMENTS/VITAMINS

SNACKS

WATER INTAKE

CALORIES   FATS   PROTEIN   CARBS

EXERCISE

DAILY REFLECTION

SLEEP

ENERGY LEVELS

DATE

Daily Journal

BREAKFAST

LUNCH

DINNER

SUPPLEMENTS/VITAMINS

SNACKS

WATER INTAKE

CALORIES   FATS   PROTEIN   CARBS

EXERCISE

DAILY REFLECTION

SLEEP

ENERGY LEVELS

DATE

Daily Journal

BREAKFAST

LUNCH

DINNER

SUPPLEMENTS/VITAMINS

SNACKS

WATER INTAKE

CALORIES   FATS   PROTEIN   CARBS

EXERCISE

DAILY REFLECTION

SLEEP

ENERGY LEVELS

DATE

Daily Journal

BREAKFAST

LUNCH

DINNER

SUPPLEMENTS/VITAMINS

SNACKS

WATER INTAKE

CALORIES   FATS   PROTEIN   CARBS

EXERCISE

DAILY REFLECTION

SLEEP

ENERGY LEVELS

DATE

Daily Journal

BREAKFAST

LUNCH

DINNER

SUPPLEMENTS/VITAMINS

SNACKS

WATER INTAKE

CALORIES   FATS   PROTEIN   CARBS

EXERCISE

DAILY REFLECTION

SLEEP

ENERGY LEVELS

Weekly Measurements Log

DATE

WEIGHT

CHEST

WAIST

BUTT

THIGHS

ARMS

HIPS

BMI

Photos During My Journey

INCLUDE PHOTOS DURING CELEBRATIONS AND MILESTONES!

Thoughts About The Week

Proud Moments

Lessons Leanred or Things I Can Do Better

Do it with passion or not at all.

DATE

Daily Journal

BREAKFAST

LUNCH

DINNER

SUPPLEMENTS/VITAMINS

SNACKS

WATER INTAKE

CALORIES   FATS   PROTEIN   CARBS

EXERCISE

DAILY REFLECTION

SLEEP

ENERGY LEVELS

DATE

Daily Journal

BREAKFAST

LUNCH

DINNER

SUPPLEMENTS/VITAMINS

SNACKS

WATER INTAKE

CALORIES   FATS   PROTEIN   CARBS

EXERCISE

DAILY REFLECTION

SLEEP

ENERGY LEVELS

DATE

Daily Journal

BREAKFAST

LUNCH

DINNER

SUPPLEMENTS/VITAMINS

SNACKS

WATER INTAKE

CALORIES   FATS   PROTEIN   CARBS

EXERCISE

DAILY REFLECTION

SLEEP

ENERGY LEVELS

DATE

Daily Journal

BREAKFAST

LUNCH

DINNER

SUPPLEMENTS/VITAMINS

SNACKS

WATER INTAKE

CALORIES   FATS   PROTEIN   CARBS

EXERCISE

DAILY REFLECTION

SLEEP

ENERGY LEVELS

DATE

Daily Journal

BREAKFAST

LUNCH

DINNER

SUPPLEMENTS/VITAMINS

SNACKS

WATER INTAKE

CALORIES   FATS   PROTEIN   CARBS

EXERCISE

DAILY REFLECTION

SLEEP

ENERGY LEVELS

DATE

Daily Journal

BREAKFAST

LUNCH

DINNER

SUPPLEMENTS/VITAMINS

SNACKS

WATER INTAKE

CALORIES   FATS   PROTEIN   CARBS

EXERCISE

DAILY REFLECTION

SLEEP

ENERGY LEVELS

DATE

Daily Journal

BREAKFAST

LUNCH

DINNER

SUPPLEMENTS/VITAMINS

SNACKS

WATER INTAKE

CALORIES   FATS   PROTEIN   CARBS

EXERCISE

DAILY REFLECTION

SLEEP

ENERGY LEVELS

Weekly Measurements Log

DATE

WEIGHT

CHEST

WAIST

BUTT

THIGHS

ARMS

HIPS

BMI

Photos During My Journey

INCLUDE PHOTOS DURING CELEBRATIONS AND MILESTONES!

Thoughts About The Week

Proud Moments

Lessons Learned or Things I Can Do Better

If you change nothing, nothing will change.

DATE

Daily Journal

BREAKFAST

LUNCH

DINNER

SUPPLEMENTS/VITAMINS

SNACKS

WATER INTAKE

CALORIES   FATS   PROTEIN   CARBS

EXERCISE

DAILY REFLECTION

SLEEP

ENERGY LEVELS

DATE

Daily Journal

BREAKFAST

LUNCH

DINNER

SUPPLEMENTS/VITAMINS

SNACKS

WATER INTAKE

CALORIES   FATS   PROTEIN   CARBS

EXERCISE

DAILY REFLECTION

SLEEP

ENERGY LEVELS

DATE

Daily Journal

BREAKFAST

LUNCH

DINNER

SUPPLEMENTS/VITAMINS

SNACKS

WATER INTAKE

CALORIES   FATS   PROTEIN   CARBS

EXERCISE

DAILY REFLECTION

SLEEP

ENERGY LEVELS

DATE

Daily Journal

BREAKFAST

LUNCH

DINNER

SUPPLEMENTS/VITAMINS

SNACKS

WATER INTAKE

CALORIES   FATS   PROTEIN   CARBS

EXERCISE

DAILY REFLECTION

SLEEP

ENERGY LEVELS

DATE

Daily Journal

BREAKFAST

LUNCH

DINNER

SUPPLEMENTS/VITAMINS

SNACKS

WATER INTAKE

CALORIES   FATS   PROTEIN   CARBS

EXERCISE

DAILY REFLECTION

SLEEP

ENERGY LEVELS

DATE

Daily Journal

BREAKFAST

LUNCH

DINNER

SUPPLEMENTS/VITAMINS

SNACKS

WATER INTAKE

CALORIES   FATS   PROTEIN   CARBS

EXERCISE

DAILY REFLECTION

SLEEP

ENERGY LEVELS

DATE

Daily Journal

BREAKFAST

LUNCH

DINNER

SUPPLEMENTS/VITAMINS

SNACKS

WATER INTAKE

CALORIES   FATS   PROTEIN   CARBS

EXERCISE

DAILY REFLECTION

SLEEP

ENERGY LEVELS

Weekly Measurements Log

DATE

WEIGHT

CHEST

WAIST

BUTT

THIGHS

ARMS

HIPS

BMI

Photos During My Journey

INCLUDE PHOTOS DURING CELEBRATIONS AND MILESTONES!

Thoughts About The Week

Proud Moments

Lessons Leanred or Things I Can Do Better

Don't blame the butter for what the bread did.

DATE

Daily Journal

BREAKFAST

LUNCH

DINNER

SUPPLEMENTS/VITAMINS

SNACKS

WATER INTAKE

CALORIES   FATS   PROTEIN   CARBS

EXERCISE

DAILY REFLECTION

SLEEP

ENERGY LEVELS

DATE

Daily Journal

BREAKFAST

LUNCH

DINNER

SUPPLEMENTS/VITAMINS

SNACKS

WATER INTAKE

CALORIES   FATS   PROTEIN   CARBS

EXERCISE

DAILY REFLECTION

SLEEP

ENERGY LEVELS

DATE

Daily Journal

BREAKFAST

LUNCH

DINNER

SUPPLEMENTS/VITAMINS

SNACKS

WATER INTAKE

CALORIES   FATS   PROTEIN   CARBS

EXERCISE

DAILY REFLECTION

SLEEP

ENERGY LEVELS

DATE

Daily Journal

BREAKFAST

LUNCH

DINNER

SUPPLEMENTS/VITAMINS

SNACKS

WATER INTAKE

CALORIES   FATS   PROTEIN   CARBS

EXERCISE

DAILY REFLECTION

SLEEP

ENERGY LEVELS

DATE

Daily Journal

BREAKFAST

LUNCH

DINNER

SUPPLEMENTS/VITAMINS

SNACKS

WATER INTAKE

CALORIES   FATS   PROTEIN   CARBS

EXERCISE

DAILY REFLECTION

SLEEP

ENERGY LEVELS

DATE

Daily Journal

BREAKFAST

LUNCH

DINNER

SUPPLEMENTS/VITAMINS

SNACKS

WATER INTAKE

CALORIES   FATS   PROTEIN   CARBS

EXERCISE

DAILY REFLECTION

SLEEP

ENERGY LEVELS

DATE

Daily Journal

BREAKFAST

LUNCH

DINNER

SUPPLEMENTS/VITAMINS

SNACKS

WATER INTAKE

CALORIES   FATS   PROTEIN   CARBS

EXERCISE

DAILY REFLECTION

SLEEP

ENERGY LEVELS

Weekly Measurements Log

DATE

WEIGHT

CHEST

WAIST

BUTT

THIGHS

ARMS

HIPS

BMI

Photos During My Journey

INCLUDE PHOTOS DURING CELEBRATIONS AND MILESTONES!

Thoughts About The Week

Proud Moments

Lessons Leanred or Things I Can Do Better

Don't stop until you're proud.

DATE

Daily Journal

BREAKFAST

LUNCH

DINNER

SUPPLEMENTS/VITAMINS

SNACKS

WATER INTAKE

CALORIES   FATS   PROTEIN   CARBS

EXERCISE

DAILY REFLECTION

SLEEP

ENERGY LEVELS

DATE

Daily Journal

BREAKFAST

LUNCH

DINNER

SUPPLEMENTS/VITAMINS

SNACKS

WATER INTAKE

CALORIES   FATS   PROTEIN   CARBS

EXERCISE

DAILY REFLECTION

SLEEP

ENERGY LEVELS

DATE

Daily Journal

BREAKFAST

LUNCH

DINNER

SUPPLEMENTS/VITAMINS

SNACKS

WATER INTAKE

CALORIES   FATS   PROTEIN   CARBS

EXERCISE

DAILY REFLECTION

SLEEP

ENERGY LEVELS

DATE

Daily Journal

BREAKFAST

LUNCH

DINNER

SUPPLEMENTS/VITAMINS

SNACKS

WATER INTAKE

CALORIES   FATS   PROTEIN   CARBS

EXERCISE

DAILY REFLECTION

SLEEP

ENERGY LEVELS

DATE

Daily Journal

BREAKFAST

LUNCH

DINNER

SUPPLEMENTS/VITAMINS

SNACKS

WATER INTAKE

CALORIES   FATS   PROTEIN   CARBS

EXERCISE

DAILY REFLECTION

SLEEP

ENERGY LEVELS

DATE

Daily Journal

BREAKFAST

LUNCH

DINNER

SUPPLEMENTS/VITAMINS

SNACKS

WATER INTAKE

CALORIES   FATS   PROTEIN   CARBS

EXERCISE

DAILY REFLECTION

SLEEP

ENERGY LEVELS

DATE

Daily Journal

BREAKFAST

LUNCH

DINNER

SUPPLEMENTS/VITAMINS

SNACKS

WATER INTAKE

CALORIES   FATS   PROTEIN   CARBS

EXERCISE

DAILY REFLECTION

SLEEP

ENERGY LEVELS

Weekly Measurements Log

DATE

WEIGHT

CHEST

WAIST

BUTT

THIGHS

ARMS

HIPS

BMI

Photos During My Journey

INCLUDE PHOTOS DURING CELEBRATIONS AND MILESTONES!

Thoughts About The Week

Proud Moments

Lessons Leanred or Things I Can Do Better

Failure is
not an option.

DATE

Daily Journal

BREAKFAST

LUNCH

DINNER

SUPPLEMENTS/VITAMINS

SNACKS

WATER INTAKE

CALORIES   FATS   PROTEIN   CARBS

EXERCISE

DAILY REFLECTION

SLEEP

ENERGY LEVELS

DATE

Daily Journal

BREAKFAST

LUNCH

DINNER

SUPPLEMENTS/VITAMINS

SNACKS

WATER INTAKE

CALORIES   FATS   PROTEIN   CARBS

EXERCISE

DAILY REFLECTION

SLEEP

ENERGY LEVELS

DATE

Daily Journal

BREAKFAST

LUNCH

DINNER

SUPPLEMENTS/VITAMINS

SNACKS

WATER INTAKE

CALORIES   FATS   PROTEIN   CARBS

EXERCISE

DAILY REFLECTION

SLEEP

ENERGY LEVELS

DATE

Daily Journal

BREAKFAST

LUNCH

DINNER

SUPPLEMENTS/VITAMINS

SNACKS

WATER INTAKE

CALORIES   FATS   PROTEIN   CARBS

EXERCISE

DAILY REFLECTION

SLEEP

ENERGY LEVELS

DATE

Daily Journal

BREAKFAST

LUNCH

DINNER

SUPPLEMENTS/VITAMINS

SNACKS

WATER INTAKE

CALORIES   FATS   PROTEIN   CARBS

EXERCISE

DAILY REFLECTION

SLEEP

ENERGY LEVELS

DATE

Daily Journal

BREAKFAST

LUNCH

DINNER

SUPPLEMENTS/VITAMINS

SNACKS

WATER INTAKE

CALORIES   FATS   PROTEIN   CARBS

EXERCISE

DAILY REFLECTION

SLEEP

ENERGY LEVELS

DATE

Daily Journal

BREAKFAST

LUNCH

DINNER

SUPPLEMENTS/VITAMINS

SNACKS

WATER INTAKE

CALORIES   FATS   PROTEIN   CARBS

EXERCISE

DAILY REFLECTION

SLEEP

ENERGY LEVELS

Weekly Measurements Log

DATE

WEIGHT

CHEST

WAIST

BUTT

THIGHS

ARMS

HIPS

BMI

Photos During My Journey

INCLUDE PHOTOS DURING CELEBRATIONS AND MILESTONES!

Thoughts About The Week

Proud Moments

Lessons Leanred or Things I Can Do Better

Life is tough, but
so are you.

DATE

Daily Journal

BREAKFAST

LUNCH

DINNER

SUPPLEMENTS/VITAMINS

SNACKS

WATER INTAKE

CALORIES   FATS   PROTEIN   CARBS

EXERCISE

DAILY REFLECTION

SLEEP

ENERGY LEVELS

DATE

Daily Journal

BREAKFAST

LUNCH

DINNER

SUPPLEMENTS/VITAMINS

SNACKS

WATER INTAKE

CALORIES   FATS   PROTEIN   CARBS

EXERCISE

DAILY REFLECTION

SLEEP

ENERGY LEVELS

DATE

Daily Journal

BREAKFAST

LUNCH

DINNER

SUPPLEMENTS/VITAMINS

SNACKS

WATER INTAKE

CALORIES   FATS   PROTEIN   CARBS

EXERCISE

DAILY REFLECTION

SLEEP

ENERGY LEVELS

DATE

Daily Journal

BREAKFAST

LUNCH

DINNER

SUPPLEMENTS/VITAMINS

SNACKS

WATER INTAKE

CALORIES   FATS   PROTEIN   CARBS

EXERCISE

DAILY REFLECTION

SLEEP

ENERGY LEVELS

DATE

Daily Journal

BREAKFAST

LUNCH

DINNER

SUPPLEMENTS/VITAMINS

SNACKS

WATER INTAKE

CALORIES   FATS   PROTEIN   CARBS

EXERCISE

DAILY REFLECTION

SLEEP

ENERGY LEVELS

DATE

Daily Journal

BREAKFAST

LUNCH

DINNER

SUPPLEMENTS/VITAMINS

SNACKS

WATER INTAKE

CALORIES   FATS   PROTEIN   CARBS

EXERCISE

DAILY REFLECTION

SLEEP

ENERGY LEVELS

DATE

Daily Journal

BREAKFAST

LUNCH

DINNER

SUPPLEMENTS/VITAMINS

SNACKS

WATER INTAKE

CALORIES   FATS   PROTEIN   CARBS

EXERCISE

DAILY REFLECTION

SLEEP

ENERGY LEVELS

Weekly Measurements Log

DATE

WEIGHT

CHEST

WAIST

BUTT

THIGHS

ARMS

HIPS

BMI

Photos During My Journey

INCLUDE PHOTOS DURING CELEBRATIONS AND MILESTONES!

Thoughts About The Week

Proud Moments

Lessons Learned or Things I Can Do Better

A little progress each day adds up to big results

DATE

Daily Journal

BREAKFAST

LUNCH

DINNER

SUPPLEMENTS/VITAMINS

SNACKS

WATER INTAKE

CALORIES   FATS   PROTEIN   CARBS

EXERCISE

DAILY REFLECTION

SLEEP

ENERGY LEVELS

DATE

Daily Journal

BREAKFAST

LUNCH

DINNER

SUPPLEMENTS/VITAMINS

SNACKS

WATER INTAKE

CALORIES   FATS   PROTEIN   CARBS

EXERCISE

DAILY REFLECTION

SLEEP

ENERGY LEVELS

DATE

Daily Journal

BREAKFAST

LUNCH

DINNER

SUPPLEMENTS/VITAMINS

SNACKS

WATER INTAKE

CALORIES   FATS   PROTEIN   CARBS

EXERCISE

DAILY REFLECTION

SLEEP

ENERGY LEVELS

DATE

Daily Journal

BREAKFAST

LUNCH

DINNER

SUPPLEMENTS/VITAMINS

SNACKS

WATER INTAKE

CALORIES   FATS   PROTEIN   CARBS

EXERCISE

DAILY REFLECTION

SLEEP

ENERGY LEVELS

DATE

Daily Journal

BREAKFAST

LUNCH

DINNER

SUPPLEMENTS/VITAMINS

SNACKS

WATER INTAKE

CALORIES   FATS   PROTEIN   CARBS

EXERCISE

DAILY REFLECTION

SLEEP

ENERGY LEVELS

DATE

Daily Journal

BREAKFAST

LUNCH

DINNER

SUPPLEMENTS/VITAMINS

SNACKS

WATER INTAKE

CALORIES   FATS   PROTEIN   CARBS

EXERCISE

DAILY REFLECTION

SLEEP

ENERGY LEVELS

DATE

Daily Journal

BREAKFAST

LUNCH

DINNER

SUPPLEMENTS/VITAMINS

SNACKS

WATER INTAKE

CALORIES   FATS   PROTEIN   CARBS

EXERCISE

DAILY REFLECTION

SLEEP

ENERGY LEVELS

Weekly Measurements Log

DATE

WEIGHT

CHEST

WAIST

BUTT

THIGHS

ARMS

HIPS

BMI

Photos During My Journey

INCLUDE PHOTOS DURING CELEBRATIONS AND MILESTONES!

Thoughts About The Week

Proud Moments

Lessons Leanred or Things I Can Do Better

Mistakes are proof that you are trying.

DATE

Daily Journal

BREAKFAST

LUNCH

DINNER

SUPPLEMENTS/VITAMINS

SNACKS

WATER INTAKE

CALORIES   FATS   PROTEIN   CARBS

EXERCISE

DAILY REFLECTION

SLEEP

ENERGY LEVELS

DATE

Daily Journal

BREAKFAST

LUNCH

DINNER

SUPPLEMENTS/VITAMINS

SNACKS

WATER INTAKE

CALORIES   FATS   PROTEIN   CARBS

EXERCISE

DAILY REFLECTION

SLEEP

ENERGY LEVELS

DATE

Daily Journal

BREAKFAST

LUNCH

DINNER

SUPPLEMENTS/VITAMINS

SNACKS

WATER INTAKE

CALORIES   FATS   PROTEIN   CARBS

EXERCISE

DAILY REFLECTION

SLEEP

ENERGY LEVELS

DATE

Daily Journal

BREAKFAST

LUNCH

DINNER

SUPPLEMENTS/VITAMINS

SNACKS

WATER INTAKE

CALORIES   FATS   PROTEIN   CARBS

EXERCISE

DAILY REFLECTION

SLEEP

ENERGY LEVELS

DATE

Daily Journal

BREAKFAST

LUNCH

DINNER

SUPPLEMENTS/VITAMINS

SNACKS

WATER INTAKE

CALORIES   FATS   PROTEIN   CARBS

EXERCISE

DAILY REFLECTION

SLEEP

ENERGY LEVELS

DATE

Daily Journal

BREAKFAST

LUNCH

DINNER

SUPPLEMENTS/VITAMINS

SNACKS

WATER INTAKE

CALORIES   FATS   PROTEIN   CARBS

EXERCISE

DAILY REFLECTION

SLEEP

ENERGY LEVELS

DATE

Daily Journal

BREAKFAST

LUNCH

DINNER

SUPPLEMENTS/VITAMINS

SNACKS

WATER INTAKE

CALORIES   FATS   PROTEIN   CARBS

EXERCISE

DAILY REFLECTION

SLEEP

ENERGY LEVELS

Weekly Measurements Log

DATE

WEIGHT

CHEST

WAIST

BUTT

THIGHS

ARMS

HIPS

BMI

Photos During My Journey

INCLUDE PHOTOS DURING CELEBRATIONS AND MILESTONES!

Thoughts About The Week

Proud Moments

Lessons Learned or Things I Can Do Better

The expert in anything was once a beginner.

DATE

Daily Journal

BREAKFAST

LUNCH

DINNER

SUPPLEMENTS/VITAMINS

SNACKS

WATER INTAKE

CALORIES   FATS   PROTEIN   CARBS

EXERCISE

DAILY REFLECTION

SLEEP

ENERGY LEVELS

DATE

Daily Journal

BREAKFAST

LUNCH

DINNER

SUPPLEMENTS/VITAMINS

SNACKS

WATER INTAKE

CALORIES   FATS   PROTEIN   CARBS

EXERCISE

DAILY REFLECTION

SLEEP

ENERGY LEVELS

DATE

Daily Journal

BREAKFAST

LUNCH

DINNER

SUPPLEMENTS/VITAMINS

SNACKS

WATER INTAKE

CALORIES   FATS   PROTEIN   CARBS

EXERCISE

DAILY REFLECTION

SLEEP

ENERGY LEVELS

DATE

Daily Journal

BREAKFAST

LUNCH

DINNER

SUPPLEMENTS/VITAMINS

SNACKS

WATER INTAKE

CALORIES   FATS   PROTEIN   CARBS

EXERCISE

DAILY REFLECTION

SLEEP

ENERGY LEVELS

DATE

Daily Journal

BREAKFAST

LUNCH

DINNER

SUPPLEMENTS/VITAMINS

SNACKS

WATER INTAKE

CALORIES   FATS   PROTEIN   CARBS

EXERCISE

DAILY REFLECTION

SLEEP

ENERGY LEVELS

DATE

Daily Journal

BREAKFAST

LUNCH

DINNER

SUPPLEMENTS/VITAMINS

SNACKS

WATER INTAKE

CALORIES   FATS   PROTEIN   CARBS

EXERCISE

DAILY REFLECTION

SLEEP

ENERGY LEVELS

DATE

Daily Journal

BREAKFAST

LUNCH

DINNER

SUPPLEMENTS/VITAMINS

SNACKS

WATER INTAKE

CALORIES   FATS   PROTEIN   CARBS

EXERCISE

DAILY REFLECTION

SLEEP

ENERGY LEVELS

Weekly Measurements Log

DATE

WEIGHT

CHEST

WAIST

BUTT

THIGHS

ARMS

HIPS

BMI

Photos During My Journey

INCLUDE PHOTOS DURING CELEBRATIONS AND MILESTONES!

Thoughts About The Week

Proud Moments

Lessons Leanred or Things I Can Do Better

It's never too early or too late to work towards being the healthiest you.

DATE

Daily Journal

BREAKFAST

LUNCH

DINNER

SUPPLEMENTS/VITAMINS

SNACKS

WATER INTAKE

CALORIES   FATS   PROTEIN   CARBS

EXERCISE

DAILY REFLECTION

SLEEP

ENERGY LEVELS

DATE

Daily Journal

BREAKFAST

LUNCH

DINNER

SUPPLEMENTS/VITAMINS

SNACKS

WATER INTAKE

CALORIES   FATS   PROTEIN   CARBS

EXERCISE

DAILY REFLECTION

SLEEP

ENERGY LEVELS

DATE

Daily Journal

BREAKFAST

LUNCH

DINNER

SUPPLEMENTS/VITAMINS

SNACKS

WATER INTAKE

CALORIES   FATS   PROTEIN   CARBS

EXERCISE

DAILY REFLECTION

SLEEP

ENERGY LEVELS

DATE

Daily Journal

BREAKFAST

LUNCH

DINNER

SUPPLEMENTS/VITAMINS

SNACKS

WATER INTAKE

CALORIES   FATS   PROTEIN   CARBS

EXERCISE

DAILY REFLECTION

SLEEP

ENERGY LEVELS

DATE

Daily Journal

BREAKFAST

LUNCH

DINNER

SUPPLEMENTS/VITAMINS

SNACKS

WATER INTAKE

CALORIES   FATS   PROTEIN   CARBS

EXERCISE

DAILY REFLECTION

SLEEP

ENERGY LEVELS

DATE

Daily Journal

BREAKFAST

LUNCH

DINNER

SUPPLEMENTS/VITAMINS

SNACKS

WATER INTAKE

CALORIES   FATS   PROTEIN   CARBS

EXERCISE

DAILY REFLECTION

SLEEP

ENERGY LEVELS

DATE

Daily Journal

BREAKFAST

LUNCH

DINNER

SUPPLEMENTS/VITAMINS

SNACKS

WATER INTAKE

CALORIES   FATS   PROTEIN   CARBS

EXERCISE

DAILY REFLECTION

SLEEP

ENERGY LEVELS

Weekly Measurements Log

DATE

WEIGHT

CHEST

WAIST

BUTT

THIGHS

ARMS

HIPS

BMI

Photos During My Journey

INCLUDE PHOTOS DURING CELEBRATIONS AND MILESTONES!

Thoughts About The Week

Proud Moments

Lessons Leanred or Things I Can Do Better

Grow through,
what you go
through.

DATE

Daily Journal

BREAKFAST

LUNCH

DINNER

SUPPLEMENTS/VITAMINS

SNACKS

WATER INTAKE

CALORIES   FATS   PROTEIN   CARBS

EXERCISE

DAILY REFLECTION

SLEEP

ENERGY LEVELS

DATE

Daily Journal

BREAKFAST

LUNCH

DINNER

SUPPLEMENTS/VITAMINS

SNACKS

WATER INTAKE

CALORIES   FATS   PROTEIN   CARBS

EXERCISE

DAILY REFLECTION

SLEEP

ENERGY LEVELS

DATE

Daily Journal

BREAKFAST

LUNCH

DINNER

SUPPLEMENTS/VITAMINS

SNACKS

WATER INTAKE

CALORIES   FATS   PROTEIN   CARBS

EXERCISE

DAILY REFLECTION

SLEEP

ENERGY LEVELS

DATE

Daily Journal

BREAKFAST

LUNCH

DINNER

SUPPLEMENTS/VITAMINS

SNACKS

WATER INTAKE

CALORIES   FATS   PROTEIN   CARBS

EXERCISE

DAILY REFLECTION

SLEEP

ENERGY LEVELS

DATE

Daily Journal

BREAKFAST

LUNCH

DINNER

SUPPLEMENTS/VITAMINS

SNACKS

WATER INTAKE

CALORIES   FATS   PROTEIN   CARBS

EXERCISE

DAILY REFLECTION

SLEEP

ENERGY LEVELS

DATE

Daily Journal

BREAKFAST

LUNCH

DINNER

SUPPLEMENTS/VITAMINS

SNACKS

WATER INTAKE

CALORIES   FATS   PROTEIN   CARBS

EXERCISE

DAILY REFLECTION

SLEEP

ENERGY LEVELS

DATE

Daily Journal

BREAKFAST

LUNCH

DINNER

SUPPLEMENTS/VITAMINS

SNACKS

WATER INTAKE

CALORIES   FATS   PROTEIN   CARBS

EXERCISE

DAILY REFLECTION

SLEEP

ENERGY LEVELS

Weekly Measurements Log

DATE

WEIGHT

CHEST

WAIST

BUTT

THIGHS

ARMS

HIPS

BMI

Photos During My Journey

INCLUDE PHOTOS DURING CELEBRATIONS AND MILESTONES!

Thoughts About The Week

Proud Moments

Lessons Leanred or Things I Can Do Better

Believe in yourself and you will be unstoppable.

DATE

Daily Journal

BREAKFAST

LUNCH

DINNER

SUPPLEMENTS/VITAMINS

SNACKS

WATER INTAKE

CALORIES   FATS   PROTEIN   CARBS

EXERCISE

DAILY REFLECTION

SLEEP

ENERGY LEVELS

DATE

Daily Journal

BREAKFAST

LUNCH

DINNER

SUPPLEMENTS/VITAMINS

SNACKS

WATER INTAKE

CALORIES   FATS   PROTEIN   CARBS

EXERCISE

DAILY REFLECTION

SLEEP

ENERGY LEVELS

DATE

Daily Journal

BREAKFAST

LUNCH

DINNER

SUPPLEMENTS/VITAMINS

SNACKS

WATER INTAKE

CALORIES   FATS   PROTEIN   CARBS

EXERCISE

DAILY REFLECTION

SLEEP

ENERGY LEVELS

DATE

Daily Journal

BREAKFAST

LUNCH

DINNER

SUPPLEMENTS/VITAMINS

SNACKS

WATER INTAKE

CALORIES   FATS   PROTEIN   CARBS

EXERCISE

DAILY REFLECTION

SLEEP

ENERGY LEVELS

DATE

Daily Journal

BREAKFAST

LUNCH

DINNER

SUPPLEMENTS/VITAMINS

SNACKS

WATER INTAKE

CALORIES   FATS   PROTEIN   CARBS

EXERCISE

DAILY REFLECTION

SLEEP

ENERGY LEVELS

DATE

Daily Journal

BREAKFAST

LUNCH

DINNER

SUPPLEMENTS/VITAMINS

SNACKS

WATER INTAKE

CALORIES   FATS   PROTEIN   CARBS

EXERCISE

DAILY REFLECTION

SLEEP

ENERGY LEVELS

DATE

Daily Journal

BREAKFAST

LUNCH

DINNER

SUPPLEMENTS/VITAMINS

SNACKS

WATER INTAKE

CALORIES   FATS   PROTEIN   CARBS

EXERCISE

DAILY REFLECTION

SLEEP

ENERGY LEVELS

Weekly Measurements Log

DATE

WEIGHT

CHEST

WAIST

BUTT

THIGHS

ARMS

HIPS

BMI

Photos During My Journey

INCLUDE PHOTOS DURING CELEBRATIONS AND MILESTONES!

Thoughts About The Week

Proud Moments

Lessons Leanred or Things I Can Do Better

Don't let a
bad day
turn into a
bad week.

DATE

Daily Journal

BREAKFAST

LUNCH

DINNER

SUPPLEMENTS/VITAMINS

SNACKS

WATER INTAKE

CALORIES   FATS   PROTEIN   CARBS

EXERCISE

DAILY REFLECTION

SLEEP

ENERGY LEVELS

DATE

Daily Journal

BREAKFAST

LUNCH

DINNER

SUPPLEMENTS/VITAMINS

SNACKS

WATER INTAKE

CALORIES   FATS   PROTEIN   CARBS

EXERCISE

DAILY REFLECTION

SLEEP

ENERGY LEVELS

DATE

Daily Journal

BREAKFAST

LUNCH

DINNER

SUPPLEMENTS/VITAMINS

SNACKS

WATER INTAKE

CALORIES   FATS   PROTEIN   CARBS

EXERCISE

DAILY REFLECTION

SLEEP

ENERGY LEVELS

DATE

Daily Journal

BREAKFAST

LUNCH

DINNER

SUPPLEMENTS/VITAMINS

SNACKS

WATER INTAKE

CALORIES   FATS   PROTEIN   CARBS

EXERCISE

DAILY REFLECTION

SLEEP

ENERGY LEVELS

DATE

Daily Journal

BREAKFAST

LUNCH

DINNER

SUPPLEMENTS/VITAMINS

SNACKS

WATER INTAKE

CALORIES   FATS   PROTEIN   CARBS

EXERCISE

DAILY REFLECTION

SLEEP

ENERGY LEVELS

DATE

Daily Journal

BREAKFAST

LUNCH

DINNER

SUPPLEMENTS/VITAMINS

SNACKS

WATER INTAKE

CALORIES   FATS   PROTEIN   CARBS

EXERCISE

DAILY REFLECTION

SLEEP

ENERGY LEVELS

DATE

Daily Journal

BREAKFAST

LUNCH

DINNER

SUPPLEMENTS/VITAMINS

SNACKS

WATER INTAKE

CALORIES   FATS   PROTEIN   CARBS

EXERCISE

DAILY REFLECTION

SLEEP

ENERGY LEVELS

Weekly Measurements Log

DATE

WEIGHT

CHEST

WAIST

BUTT

THIGHS

ARMS

HIPS

BMI

Photos During My Journey

INCLUDE PHOTOS DURING CELEBRATIONS AND MILESTONES!

Thoughts About The Week

Proud Moments

Lessons Learned or Things I Can Do Better

Eat less sugar.
You are sweet
enough already.

DATE

Daily Journal

BREAKFAST

LUNCH

DINNER

SUPPLEMENTS/VITAMINS

SNACKS

WATER INTAKE

CALORIES   FATS   PROTEIN   CARBS

EXERCISE

DAILY REFLECTION

SLEEP

ENERGY LEVELS

DATE

Daily Journal

BREAKFAST

LUNCH

DINNER

SUPPLEMENTS/VITAMINS

SNACKS

WATER INTAKE

CALORIES   FATS   PROTEIN   CARBS

EXERCISE

DAILY REFLECTION

SLEEP

ENERGY LEVELS

DATE

Daily Journal

BREAKFAST

LUNCH

DINNER

SUPPLEMENTS/VITAMINS

SNACKS

WATER INTAKE

CALORIES   FATS   PROTEIN   CARBS

EXERCISE

DAILY REFLECTION

SLEEP

ENERGY LEVELS

DATE

Daily Journal

BREAKFAST

LUNCH

DINNER

SUPPLEMENTS/VITAMINS

SNACKS

WATER INTAKE

CALORIES   FATS   PROTEIN   CARBS

EXERCISE

DAILY REFLECTION

SLEEP

ENERGY LEVELS

DATE

Daily Journal

BREAKFAST

LUNCH

DINNER

SUPPLEMENTS/VITAMINS

SNACKS

WATER INTAKE

CALORIES   FATS   PROTEIN   CARBS

EXERCISE

DAILY REFLECTION

SLEEP

ENERGY LEVELS

DATE

Daily Journal

BREAKFAST

LUNCH

DINNER

SUPPLEMENTS/VITAMINS

SNACKS

WATER INTAKE

CALORIES   FATS   PROTEIN   CARBS

EXERCISE

DAILY REFLECTION

SLEEP

ENERGY LEVELS

DATE

Daily Journal

BREAKFAST

LUNCH

DINNER

SUPPLEMENTS/VITAMINS

SNACKS

WATER INTAKE

CALORIES   FATS   PROTEIN   CARBS

EXERCISE

DAILY REFLECTION

SLEEP

ENERGY LEVELS

Weekly Measurements Log

DATE

WEIGHT

CHEST

WAIST

BUTT

THIGHS

ARMS

HIPS

BMI

Photos During My Journey

INCLUDE PHOTOS DURING CELEBRATIONS AND MILESTONES!

Thoughts About The Week

Proud Moments

Lessons Leanred or Things I Can Do Better

It's not about having time, it's about making time.

DATE

Daily Journal

BREAKFAST

LUNCH

DINNER

SUPPLEMENTS/VITAMINS

SNACKS

WATER INTAKE

CALORIES   FATS   PROTEIN   CARBS

EXERCISE

DAILY REFLECTION

SLEEP

ENERGY LEVELS

DATE

Daily Journal

BREAKFAST

LUNCH

DINNER

SUPPLEMENTS/VITAMINS

SNACKS

WATER INTAKE

CALORIES   FATS   PROTEIN   CARBS

EXERCISE

DAILY REFLECTION

SLEEP

ENERGY LEVELS

DATE

Daily Journal

BREAKFAST

LUNCH

DINNER

SUPPLEMENTS/VITAMINS

SNACKS

WATER INTAKE

CALORIES   FATS   PROTEIN   CARBS

EXERCISE

DAILY REFLECTION

SLEEP

ENERGY LEVELS

DATE

Daily Journal

BREAKFAST

LUNCH

DINNER

SUPPLEMENTS/VITAMINS

SNACKS

WATER INTAKE

CALORIES   FATS   PROTEIN   CARBS

EXERCISE

DAILY REFLECTION

SLEEP

ENERGY LEVELS

DATE

Daily Journal

BREAKFAST

LUNCH

DINNER

SUPPLEMENTS/VITAMINS

SNACKS

WATER INTAKE

CALORIES   FATS   PROTEIN   CARBS

EXERCISE

DAILY REFLECTION

SLEEP

ENERGY LEVELS

DATE

Daily Journal

BREAKFAST

LUNCH

DINNER

SUPPLEMENTS/VITAMINS

SNACKS

WATER INTAKE

CALORIES   FATS   PROTEIN   CARBS

EXERCISE

DAILY REFLECTION

SLEEP

ENERGY LEVELS

DATE

Daily Journal

BREAKFAST

LUNCH

DINNER

SUPPLEMENTS/VITAMINS

SNACKS

WATER INTAKE

CALORIES   FATS   PROTEIN   CARBS

EXERCISE

DAILY REFLECTION

SLEEP

ENERGY LEVELS

Weekly Measurements Log

DATE

WEIGHT

CHEST

WAIST

BUTT

THIGHS

ARMS

HIPS

BMI

Photos During My Journey

INCLUDE PHOTOS DURING CELEBRATIONS AND MILESTONES!

Thoughts About The Week

Proud Moments

Lessons Leanred or Things I Can Do Better

I'm not dieting.
I'm changing my
lifestyle.

DATE

Daily Journal

BREAKFAST

LUNCH

DINNER

SUPPLEMENTS/VITAMINS

SNACKS

WATER INTAKE

CALORIES   FATS   PROTEIN   CARBS

EXERCISE

DAILY REFLECTION

SLEEP

ENERGY LEVELS

DATE

Daily Journal

BREAKFAST

LUNCH

DINNER

SUPPLEMENTS/VITAMINS

SNACKS

WATER INTAKE

CALORIES   FATS   PROTEIN   CARBS

EXERCISE

DAILY REFLECTION

SLEEP

ENERGY LEVELS

DATE

Daily Journal

BREAKFAST

LUNCH

DINNER

SUPPLEMENTS/VITAMINS

SNACKS

WATER INTAKE

CALORIES   FATS   PROTEIN   CARBS

EXERCISE

DAILY REFLECTION

SLEEP

ENERGY LEVELS

DATE

Daily Journal

BREAKFAST

LUNCH

DINNER

SUPPLEMENTS/VITAMINS

SNACKS

WATER INTAKE

CALORIES   FATS   PROTEIN   CARBS

EXERCISE

DAILY REFLECTION

SLEEP

ENERGY LEVELS

DATE

Daily Journal

BREAKFAST

LUNCH

DINNER

SUPPLEMENTS/VITAMINS

SNACKS

WATER INTAKE

CALORIES   FATS   PROTEIN   CARBS

EXERCISE

DAILY REFLECTION

SLEEP

ENERGY LEVELS

DATE

Daily Journal

BREAKFAST

LUNCH

DINNER

SUPPLEMENTS/VITAMINS

SNACKS

WATER INTAKE

CALORIES   FATS   PROTEIN   CARBS

EXERCISE

DAILY REFLECTION

SLEEP

ENERGY LEVELS

DATE

Daily Journal

BREAKFAST

LUNCH

DINNER

SUPPLEMENTS/VITAMINS

SNACKS

WATER INTAKE

CALORIES   FATS   PROTEIN   CARBS

EXERCISE

DAILY REFLECTION

SLEEP

ENERGY LEVELS

Weekly Measurements Log

DATE

WEIGHT

CHEST

WAIST

BUTT

THIGHS

ARMS

HIPS

BMI

Photos During My Journey

INCLUDE PHOTOS DURING CELEBRATIONS AND MILESTONES!

Thoughts About The Week

Proud Moments

Lessons Leanred or Things I Can Do Better

Stay patient
and trust your
journey.

DATE

Daily Journal

BREAKFAST

LUNCH

DINNER

SUPPLEMENTS/VITAMINS

SNACKS

WATER INTAKE

CALORIES   FATS   PROTEIN   CARBS

EXERCISE

DAILY REFLECTION

SLEEP

ENERGY LEVELS

DATE

Daily Journal

BREAKFAST

LUNCH

DINNER

SUPPLEMENTS/VITAMINS

SNACKS

WATER INTAKE

CALORIES   FATS   PROTEIN   CARBS

EXERCISE

DAILY REFLECTION

SLEEP

ENERGY LEVELS

DATE

Daily Journal

BREAKFAST

LUNCH

DINNER

SUPPLEMENTS/VITAMINS

SNACKS

WATER INTAKE

CALORIES   FATS   PROTEIN   CARBS

EXERCISE

DAILY REFLECTION

SLEEP

ENERGY LEVELS

DATE

Daily Journal

BREAKFAST

LUNCH

DINNER

SUPPLEMENTS/VITAMINS

SNACKS

WATER INTAKE

CALORIES   FATS   PROTEIN   CARBS

EXERCISE

DAILY REFLECTION

SLEEP

ENERGY LEVELS

DATE

Daily Journal

BREAKFAST

LUNCH

DINNER

SUPPLEMENTS/VITAMINS

SNACKS

WATER INTAKE

CALORIES   FATS   PROTEIN   CARBS

EXERCISE

DAILY REFLECTION

SLEEP

ENERGY LEVELS

DATE

Daily Journal

BREAKFAST

LUNCH

DINNER

SUPPLEMENTS/VITAMINS

SNACKS

WATER INTAKE

CALORIES   FATS   PROTEIN   CARBS

EXERCISE

DAILY REFLECTION

SLEEP

ENERGY LEVELS

DATE

Daily Journal

BREAKFAST

LUNCH

DINNER

SUPPLEMENTS/VITAMINS

SNACKS

WATER INTAKE

CALORIES   FATS   PROTEIN   CARBS

EXERCISE

DAILY REFLECTION

SLEEP

ENERGY LEVELS

Weekly Measurements Log

DATE

WEIGHT

CHEST

WAIST

BUTT

THIGHS

ARMS

HIPS

BMI

Photos During My Journey

INCLUDE PHOTOS DURING CELEBRATIONS AND MILESTONES!

Thoughts About The Week

Proud Moments

Lessons Leanred or Things I Can Do Better

If the plan doesn't work, change the plan but never the goal.

DATE

Daily Journal

BREAKFAST

LUNCH

DINNER

SUPPLEMENTS/VITAMINS

SNACKS

WATER INTAKE

CALORIES   FATS   PROTEIN   CARBS

EXERCISE

DAILY REFLECTION

SLEEP

ENERGY LEVELS

DATE

Daily Journal

BREAKFAST

LUNCH

DINNER

SUPPLEMENTS/VITAMINS

SNACKS

WATER INTAKE

CALORIES   FATS   PROTEIN   CARBS

EXERCISE

DAILY REFLECTION

SLEEP

ENERGY LEVELS

DATE

Daily Journal

BREAKFAST

LUNCH

DINNER

SUPPLEMENTS/VITAMINS

SNACKS

WATER INTAKE

CALORIES   FATS   PROTEIN   CARBS

EXERCISE

DAILY REFLECTION

SLEEP

ENERGY LEVELS

DATE

Daily Journal

BREAKFAST

LUNCH

DINNER

SUPPLEMENTS/VITAMINS

SNACKS

WATER INTAKE

CALORIES   FATS   PROTEIN   CARBS

EXERCISE

DAILY REFLECTION

SLEEP

ENERGY LEVELS

DATE

Daily Journal

BREAKFAST

LUNCH

DINNER

SUPPLEMENTS/VITAMINS

SNACKS

WATER INTAKE

CALORIES   FATS   PROTEIN   CARBS

EXERCISE

DAILY REFLECTION

SLEEP

ENERGY LEVELS

DATE

Daily Journal

BREAKFAST

LUNCH

DINNER

SUPPLEMENTS/VITAMINS

SNACKS

WATER INTAKE

CALORIES   FATS   PROTEIN   CARBS

EXERCISE

DAILY REFLECTION

SLEEP

ENERGY LEVELS

DATE

Daily Journal

BREAKFAST

LUNCH

DINNER

SUPPLEMENTS/VITAMINS

SNACKS

WATER INTAKE

CALORIES   FATS   PROTEIN   CARBS

EXERCISE

DAILY REFLECTION

SLEEP

ENERGY LEVELS

Weekly Measurements Log

DATE

WEIGHT

CHEST

WAIST

BUTT

THIGHS

ARMS

HIPS

BMI

Photos During My Journey

INCLUDE PHOTOS DURING CELEBRATIONS AND MILESTONES!

Thoughts About The Week

Proud Moments

Lessons Leanred or Things I Can Do Better

You don't need to be perfect. Just be better than you were yesterday.

DATE

Daily Journal

BREAKFAST

LUNCH

DINNER

SUPPLEMENTS/VITAMINS

SNACKS

WATER INTAKE

CALORIES   FATS   PROTEIN   CARBS

EXERCISE

DAILY REFLECTION

SLEEP

ENERGY LEVELS

DATE

Daily Journal

BREAKFAST

LUNCH

DINNER

SUPPLEMENTS/VITAMINS

SNACKS

WATER INTAKE

CALORIES   FATS   PROTEIN   CARBS

EXERCISE

DAILY REFLECTION

SLEEP

ENERGY LEVELS

DATE

Daily Journal

BREAKFAST

LUNCH

DINNER

SUPPLEMENTS/VITAMINS

SNACKS

WATER INTAKE

CALORIES   FATS   PROTEIN   CARBS

EXERCISE

DAILY REFLECTION

SLEEP

ENERGY LEVELS

DATE

Daily Journal

BREAKFAST

LUNCH

DINNER

SUPPLEMENTS/VITAMINS

SNACKS

WATER INTAKE

CALORIES   FATS   PROTEIN   CARBS

EXERCISE

DAILY REFLECTION

SLEEP

ENERGY LEVELS

DATE

Daily Journal

BREAKFAST

LUNCH

DINNER

SUPPLEMENTS/VITAMINS

SNACKS

WATER INTAKE

CALORIES   FATS   PROTEIN   CARBS

EXERCISE

DAILY REFLECTION

SLEEP

ENERGY LEVELS

DATE

Daily Journal

BREAKFAST

LUNCH

DINNER

SUPPLEMENTS/VITAMINS

SNACKS

WATER INTAKE

CALORIES   FATS   PROTEIN   CARBS

EXERCISE

DAILY REFLECTION

SLEEP

ENERGY LEVELS

DATE

Daily Journal

BREAKFAST

LUNCH

DINNER

SUPPLEMENTS/VITAMINS

SNACKS

WATER INTAKE

CALORIES   FATS   PROTEIN   CARBS

EXERCISE

DAILY REFLECTION

SLEEP

ENERGY LEVELS

Weekly Measurements Log

DATE

WEIGHT

CHEST

WAIST

BUTT

THIGHS

ARMS

HIPS

BMI

Photos During My Journey

INCLUDE PHOTOS DURING CELEBRATIONS AND MILESTONES!

Thoughts About The Week

Proud Moments

Lessons Leanred or Things I Can Do Better

Nothing tastes as good as healthy feels.

Manufactured by Amazon.ca
Bolton, ON